Contents

Designed by Michele Charles Barnes

INTRODUCTION FROM PETER AND CHERYL BARNES

Dear Teachers, Students and Friends,

We have been writing books together since 1993, when we published our first work about a cat named Nat. Since then, mice have become our favorite characters, and we have created many of them for our books for children about the three branches of government. They live in an imaginary country that parallels our own, the United Mice of America. And like us, the mice have a President, Woodrow G. Washingtail; a Speaker of the House (in our books, a "Squeaker,"), Longworth McMouse; a Senate Majority (or "Mouse-jority") Leader, Russell Mouse Bennett, and a Chief Justice of the Supreme Court, Marshall J. Mouse. Not surprisingly, their government operates just like ours, with the same rules, benefits and challenges.

We began writing about government quite by accident. We happen to live in the Washington, D.C., area and had written books about special and historic places around the country. In 1994, a friend suggested that we write a book for young readers about the White House, which is certainly a special and historic place. We thought it was a good idea and proceeded with *Woodrow, the White House Mouse*. When the book came out in 1995, Woodrow quickly became a popular fellow. Our friends in education said books on the two other branches of government would give them a series they could use in classrooms. *House Mouse, Senate Mouse*, about Congress and the legislative process, followed in 1996, and *Marshall, the Courthouse Mouse*, about law and the Supreme Court, was published in 1998.

Why mice characters? The concepts we are trying to get across to children are difficult even for many adults to grasp. By using warm, friendly, fuzzy mice in fun stories, we can educate children about these concepts in a positive, interesting way that keeps their attention.

And teach them we must. In an age of growing cynicism of our national institutions and growing apathy toward civic responsibility, children must learn early on about their government in a positive way, to start preparing them for good citizenship and participation. We want them interested in issues and politics when they are young so that when they grow up, they will read, debate, vote, care, become active in their communities and perhaps run for political office themselves – for school board, city council, judge, state representative, Congress or even the White House! Perhaps one day, years from now, a President will reveal to the world that he or she was inspired to run for office by *Woodrow, the White House Mouse!*

Happy learning and mousefully yours,

Peter and Cheryl Barnes

OVERVIEW OF CURRICULUM

Woodrow, the White House Mouse; House Mouse, Senate Mouse and Marshall, the Courthouse Mouse offer an opportunity to explain the three branches of United States government through picture books suitable for multi-grade levels. The books also offer students an overview of the art and architecture of the White House, the Capitol and the Supreme Court in Washington, D.C.

The books use rhyming verse, friendly mouse characters and colorful illustrations of the White House, Congress and the Supreme Court to pull children into the material, to entertain them and to keep their attention. The historical notes included in each book provide additional information and fun facts, and they serve as a springboard for further study and investigation.

Before students read the books, teachers should give them an overview of the basic structure of the U.S. government. The historical notes at the end of each book supply an overview. Also see Appendix 26 for a chart of the structure. The book notes are summarized here:

After the United States became independent from England in 1783, the Founding Fathers did not want another king, with unchecked power, to run the young country. So in the Constitution, they divided power among three equal branches of government: The legislative (Congress), the executive (President) and the judicial (Supreme Court). The idea was to create a system of "checks and balances," with no one branch dominating the other. To make changes and get things done, there had to be general agreement among all three branches. Taken together, the books show the branches' interaction. Each book also outlines the responsibilities of each branch, as established in the Constitution. Use Appendix 26, a chart of the structure, as a teaching aid.

The Constitution gives Congress the sole power to create laws. Congress is made up of two "chambers," the House of Representatives and the Senate. The House is the larger chamber, with 435 members elected for two-year terms; the Senate has 100 members elected for six-year terms. The Founding Fathers created two bodies to ensure a balance of power between large states and small states. Because each state has two members in the Senate, a small state like Delaware has a vote equal to a big state like California and thus has as much power. This structure forces the House and Senate to negotiate and compromise on every piece of proposed legislation. This helps to protect the rights of small states and their citizens.

The President is the nation's "Chief Executive." He runs the government, enforcing laws and directing the many departments and agencies that implement them. Though he doesn't have any direct power to make laws, he works with Congress on crafting laws, making recommendations for legislation that Congress can then consider or dismiss. The Constitution also gives him a major role in creating laws by giving him final approval or rejection (veto) of proposed laws after they have passed Congress. The President also works with leaders of other countries, negotiating treaties and agreements. In this capacity, the President acts as "Head of State." As Head of State, he also is expected to be America's biggest cheerleader, upholding its traditions, dedicating monuments, presenting awards and participating in other ceremonial functions at home and abroad. Finally, the Constitution says the President is the "Commander in Chief" of the nation's military.

The Supreme Court is the highest court in the land. Its main responsibility is to settle the nation's most complex legal disputes and constitutional questions. In this capacity, it often must interpret the Constitution and tries to determine what the Founding Fathers intended when they wrote the document more than 200 years ago. The Court is often required to settle disagreements between the two other branches of government, Congress and the President; it also settles major legal conflicts between states. But typically, the Court is the last judicial body to hear a case. A case first must wind its way through the lower courts, and even then, it will reach the "High Court" only if at least four of the nine justices agree it is important enough to deserve the Court's attention.

Key Points to Cover:

★ The U.S. government is divided into three separate branches.

★ The three branches are the legislative (Congress), the executive (President) and the judicial (Supreme Court). The Congress is further divided into two separate chambers, the House of Representatives and the Senate.

★ The Constitution gives each branch specific powers and responsibilities.

★ The government is divided to assure that no one group or person, such as a king or the military, has total power over the nation. This division of power helps assure freedom, fairness, justice and equal treatment for all citizens.

About the Authors

Cheryl Shaw Barnes is a self-taught artist who was born and raised in Alexandria, Va. She graduated from Randolph-Macon Woman's College with a bachelor's degree in political science. After working in the Washington, D.C., area, she moved to Los Angeles, where she co-founded an architecture firm. There she developed the love and appreciation for architecture reflected in her books. She and her family returned to Virginia in 1990.

Cheryl became an illustrator because she became ill one day. While in bed with the flu, she decided to doodle some pictures for a book she and Peter were planning to write, *Alexander, the Old Town Mouse*. She kept her drawings hidden from her family. She included one of her illustrations in a pile of artwork from other artists who wanted to draw Alexander. Peter thought the drawing was very good and asked Cheryl who had submitted it. To Peter's surprise, Cheryl announced she had! *Alexander* went on to become Cheryl's first book.

"I never thought I would have a career as a children's book illustrator and writer," Cheryl said. "It truly is a wonderful job. And all because I got the flu one day!"

Among other books, she has illustrated and co-authored *Woodrow, the White House Mouse*; *House Mouse, Senate Mouse* and *Marshall, the Courthouse Mouse*. She is an honorary member of Delta Kappa Gamma, a teachers sorority, and a member of the board of Northern Virginia Reading Is Fundamental.

Peter Barnes is a Washington-based broadcaster and journalist who has worked for CNBC, FOX television and the *Wall Street Journal*, among other news organizations. In 1997, he won an Ace Award, the cable television industry's highest honor, for a documentary on America's retirement system. He was born in Rochester, N.Y., and raised in Philadelphia, Pa. He graduated from Penn State University with a bachelor's degree in political science and earned a master's degree in finance from the University of Pennsylvania's Wharton School.

"My experience as a reporter in Washington, D.C., gave me a good understanding of the workings of government and lots of good material for our books," Peter said.

The Barneses have met many members of Congress, as well as several Presidents and First Ladies. They have also visited the White House, the Capitol and the Supreme Court on many occasions. They have two children and live in Alexandria.

Learning about the Presidency and the White House with *Woodrow, the White House Mouse*

Story Synopsis

Woodrow, the White House Mouse* is about an imaginary society of mice in the United States with a government that operates like our own. Just as we elect a president, it elects a mouse President every four years. In the last mouse election, Woodrow G. Washingtail won the presidency. Like his human counterpart, he is sworn into office on Inauguration Day, January 20. According to tradition, Woodrow attends the Inaugural Ball at the White House that evening. Woodrow arrives with his First Lady, Bess, and their eight children. At the same time, the human occupants of the mansion are celebrating the election of their President. The book's tour of the White House begins during this celebration, in the State Room, where Woodrow's children are already causing mischief.

Woodrow settles into work in the Oval Office. The President has a big job with many responsibilities: He must work with Congress on creating legislation; he is in charge of running the operations of government through the various agencies and departments; he is the Commander in Chief of the armed forces; and he is the nation's Head of State.

But the position of President is not all work. He and the First Lady sponsor the annual Easter Egg Roll on the South Lawn. They host artistic events in the East Room. Woodrow also takes time out to play with his children in the historic rooms of the White House, such as the Red Room and Green Room.

Perhaps the most special time in the mansion is winter holidays, when the Blue Room is the site of the White House Christmas tree. In this family setting, Woodrow considers his fun and work, and his good fortune at being elected to the highest office in the (mouse) land. He muses about running for re-election.

The last two pages of the book are historical notes for parents and teachers. They include a basic overview of the presidency, some fun facts about Presidents, and information on the construction and architecture of the White House.

Before Reading

Teachers should tell students that they will be reading about a President Mouse! Be sure to explain that this mouse is <u>imaginary</u>, that he and his world exist only in our minds. But explain that by reading about Woodrow and his family, students will learn about the job of the President and about his special home, the White House in Washington, D.C.

Teachers can also prepare for the story by asking students what they already know about the presidency: Who is the current President? What is his job? Where does he live? When was he elected? Who was elected the first President?

Teachers can also discuss the author and illustrator, Peter and Cheryl Barnes, their books and backgrounds. Teachers can point out that the Barneses live outside of Washington, D.C., have met Presidents and First Ladies and been to the White House many times. In fact, Peter was a television news reporter who once covered the White House as part of his job.

Teachers should also be sure to tell students to study the detailed illustrations in the story, which are historically accurate, and should alert students to listen for the rhyme and rhythm of the text.

During Reading

It is important that *Woodrow* be read aloud to students so that they can listen to the rhyme and rhythm of the words as well as attend to the story line.

Re-reading

Re-read the book to the entire class or small groups OR use multiple copies of the book and have students read in small groups so that each student can work with a copy of the book. For older students, partner reading may be appropriate.

A second read-aloud session is suggested with a specific focus for the listeners, either for the entire class or for cooperative learning groups. Possible <u>focus</u> directions are:

★ How does a person become President?
★ What are the President's four major responsibilities?
★ What are the names of some of the government departments the President oversees?
★ When does the President have the opportunity to have fun at the White House?
★ What are the major rooms of the White House?
  • In which room does the President do most of his work?
  • In that room, what are the important furnishings that symbolize the President's authority?
  • What room is used for official dinners?
  • What room is used for entertaining?

After Reading

Help students brainstorm a list of what they have learned about the President and the White House. These facts may be recorded by students on the "Facts" sheet (see Appendix 3). Work with students to create an outline of the facts, grouping ideas that belong together. Give each group of facts a heading and put them in logical order to create an outline. Possible headings include the President's job, rooms of the White House and how they are used, etc. Other headings will be initiated by students' ideas.

After students have created their outlines, help students summarize the information. Facts can be presented in organized presentations that include the most important points learned. Presentations can be a group project or individual effort, oral or written, and prepared in a variety of ways. The final product may include reports, charts or graphs, dramatization, audio/visual format, etc.

Generate a list of questions still to be answered and/or ideas for further research.

Activities

These suggested activities can be done by students individually, in cooperative groups and/or by the whole class. Select the activities most appropriate for your grade level and students. All appendices may be reproduced on paper, transparency or any other classroom medium.

1. Character Study

★ Write a character sketch using adjectives to describe Woodrow.

★ Use a "Descriptive Organizer" for Woodrow (see Appendix 4).

★ List main character and supporting characters.

★ Use a "Character Study Organizer" to list character traits and important events related to Woodrow (see Appendix 5).

★ Compare and contrast Woodrow with a different character from another book, using the "Compare/Contrast Organizer" (see Appendix 6).

2. Charts and Diagrams

★ Make a chart or diagram of the President's different jobs.

★ Make a chart or diagram of some of the rooms of the White House.

★ Complete a "Story Map" for the book (choose Appendix 7 or 8).

★ Retell the story using the "Sequential Organizer," "Step by Step" or "Sequence Chain" to list main or important events (see Appendices 16, 17 & 18).

★ Identify the different departments of government that report to the President (see Appendix 2 or complete crossword puzzle on Appendix 20).

★ Complete the Woodrow crossword puzzle (see Appendix 22).

3. Poetry and writing

★ Write a rhyming poem about mice or a poem with a mouse character.

★ Write an Acrostic poem, using words like "mouse," "President" or "Woodrow"
(see Appendix 9 for sample).

★ Write a Diamante (Diamond) poem, a Cinquain or a free form poem, using words generated
from the book (See Appendices 10 & 11 for samples).

★ Make a list of words describing the President. Use these words to write a patriotic poem.

4. Drawing

★ Draw a mouse character (see Appendices 12, 13 & 14).

★ Make a mouse bookmark (see Appendix 15).

★ Draw a cartoon with mice characters. Older students can learn about political cartoons
and create their own. Younger students will enjoy creating a cartoon for the comic
section of the sunday newspaper.

5. Discourse

★ Develop arguments to persuade the President to sign or veto a bill. Students
can use the "Pro/Con Organizer" to formulate a list of arguments (see Appendix 19).

★ Hold a mock presidential debate with students playing two or more competing candidates,
a moderator and questioners.

★ Hold a mock election. Include campaign speeches, promotional signs, candidates' television
commercials, etc. Create paper ballots and set up ballot boxes to allow students to cast votes.

*Note: Teachers may want to create a one-or two-week module out of the role-playing
exercise suggested above.*

6. Correspondence

★ Write a letter to the President about an important issue.

★ Write the First Lady.

The address for the President and First Lady is:
The White House
1600 Pennsylvania Avenue NW
Washington, D.C. 20500

*Note to teachers: As a matter of policy, the White House usually responds to every letter sent to the
President, First Lady or a member of the first family.*

★ Choose a cabinet department, such as the Department of Education, and write the secretary of
that department for information about its function (see cabinet addresses in Appendix 1).

7. *News*

★ Write a news story about a new bill passed by Congress and signed into law by the President.

★ Prepare a news bulletin for a television news broadcast.

★ Prepare a list of questions for a one-on-one interview with the President.

★ Hold a mock presidential press conference. Student reporters should prepare appropriate questions to ask. (For instructional purposes, teachers may want to show a videotape of a presidential press conference or have students watch one in a live television broadcast.)

★ Keep a journal or folder of news reports about the President for a period of time. Students must use newspapers, magazines and other print resources. Organize the articles according to the President's four major responsibilities outlined in the book. Students can do this individually or in groups.

8. *Suggested Research Topics*

★ Research the job of the President as described in the Constitution (Article II).

★ Learn more about the current President, his family and administration.

★ Research the meaning of the Presidential Seal.

★ Research the history of the Resolute Desk in the Oval Office.

★ Research the history of the White House Easter Egg Roll.

★ Research the history of the White House.

★ Research the history of the Inaugural Ball. In early years, there used to be one ball (at the White House) to celebrate the inauguration of a President. Today, there are many balls held in Washington when a President is sworn into office.

★ Research the history of one of the major rooms in the White House. Compare the drawing of that room in the book to an actual photograph of the room. How is it the same as the drawing? How is it different from the drawing?

★ Research a child of a President, such as:

      Caroline Kennedy

      Amy Carter

      Ruth Cleveland

      Chelsea Clinton

      Julie Nixon Eisenhower

      John F. Kennedy Jr.

      Lynda Johnson Robb

      Quentin Roosevelt

      Kermit Roosevelt

      Margaret Truman

9. Select a past President to learn more about. In addition to standard research sources, students might use the National Geographic CD-ROM program, *The Presidents – It All Started with George*.

10. Select a past First Lady to learn more about. For example, in the book, Bess is named for Bess Truman, wife of President Harry Truman. Here are some other famous First Ladies:

> Mary Todd Lincoln
> Dolley Madison
> Jacqueline Kennedy Onassis
> Eleanor Roosevelt
> Martha Custis Washington

11. Research important days that relate to the book and the presidency, such as Presidents' Day, Election Day and Flag Day.

12. As an individual exercise, each student can prepare an oral or written presentation on what he or she would do if he or she were President. The report should include major issues in society the student would address as President.

13. As an individual exercise, students may respond to the book using the "Pro/Con Organizer" to list reasons why they like or dislike the book (see Appendix 19).

14. Research Washington, D.C., the nation's capital. In every nation, the capital is a special place. It is usually full of unique and historic buildings, representing the best architecture of a nation. Identify the special buildings in Washington, D.C. Compare Washington to your town or city, or to your county seat or state capital. Use photographs from newspapers, magazines or books. What are the special buildings in your town, city, county seat or state capital?

Note to teachers: You may consider organizing a field trip to the important buildings in your locality, or to your county seat or state capital to supplement this research. You may also want to compare only one Washington structure with the corresponding structure in your community, such as the White House with City Hall, the Supreme Court with the county courthouse, etc.

For all research projects, encourage students to use a variety of sources, including books, magazines, newspapers, special reference materials, historical records, personal tours/interviews, brochures, the Internet, CD-ROMs, E-mail contacts, etc.

Check for Understanding

By the end of study of *Woodrow, the White House Mouse*, students should know:

> ★ the four major responsibilities of the President.
> ★ how a person becomes President.
> ★ some of the important rooms in the White House and how they are used.
> ★ some of the events that are held at the White House.

Glossary

Bill – a proposed law.

Congress – the legislative branch of the federal government, consisting of the House of Representatives and the Senate.

Commander in Chief – the President as the civilian leader of the nation's military forces.

Constitution – the plan of government adopted by Founding Fathers that establishes the basic law and structure of the U.S. government.

Department – a division of the executive branch of government that represents and oversees a major sector of the economy (agriculture, energy, etc.) and/or a specific responsibility of government (defense, education, etc.).

Election and re-election – the process of selecting by vote a person (candidate) for a position or office.

Foreign – from outside one's own nation.

Inauguration – a ceremony to formally swear in or induct an elected official into a public office.

Head of State – the President as the nation's chief representative to foreign countries and as the ceremonial leader of the U.S.

House – the House of Representatives, the "lower" chamber of Congress, with 435 members elected for two-year terms.

Law – a rule of conduct or behavior formally recognized by a society and enforced by legal authorities.

President – (from the Latin praesidens) the leader of the executive branch of the U.S. government, with responsibility for the operation of government departments and offices.

Senate – the "upper" chamber of Congress, with 100 members elected for six-year terms.

Veto – in the presidency, the act of formally rejecting a piece of proposed legislation already passed by Congress, which can override a veto by a two-thirds vote.

Websites

www.4government.com

An all-purpose website for the different branches of government. It includes links to most major websites for the three main branches, as well as additional links to major government departments and agencies (under "Executive Branch"), to state and local government sites, and to sites for major historical documents, including the Constitution and the Bill of Rights. It also offers links to international governing institutions, such as the United Nations.

www.4president.com

Part of the 4Government website, it offers kids (and grownups) lots of presidential information and news. It includes profiles of all the presidents and First Ladies, as well as links to the White House website and the website for the White House Historical Society.

www.whitehouse.gov/WH/kids/html/kidshome.html

The webpage on the White House website for kids.

www.whitehousehistory.org

The website of the White House Historical Society. It includes information on the history of the mansion. It also offers a webpage for kids.

www.nara.gov

The website of the National Archives (formally known as the National Archives and Record Administration). It offers access to many federal documents, but the main attraction for kids is the Online Exhibition Hall, which includes the Constitution, the Bill of Rights and the Declaration of Independence. There is also a Digital Classroom.

Bibliography/Resources, Related-Reading

Aikman, Lonnelle. The Living White House. Washington, DC: The White House Historical Association, 1991.

Arbelbide, C.L. The White House Easter Egg Roll. Washington, DC: The White House Historical Association, 1997.

Beckman, Beatrice. I Can Be President. Chicago: Childrens Press, 1984.

Blue, Rose, and Corinne J. Naden. The White House Kids. Brookfield, CN: The Millbrook Press, 1995.

Debnam, Betty. <u>A Kid's Guide to the White House</u>. Kansas City, KS: Andrews McMeel Publishing, 1997.

Fisher, Leonard Everett. <u>The White House</u>. New York: Holiday House, 1989.

Flitner, David. <u>Those People in Washington</u>. Chicago: Childrens Press, 1973.

Fradin, Dennis B. <u>Voting and Elections</u>. Chicago: Childrens Press, 1985.

Freidel, Frank. <u>The Presidents of the United States of America</u>. Washington, DC: White House Historical Association with the cooperation of the National Geographic Society, 1995.

Goldberg, Judy. Editor. <u>Dear Chelsea</u>. New York: Scholastic, 1994.

Greene, Carol. <u>Presidents</u>. Chicago: Childrens Press, 1993.

Guzzetti, Paula. <u>The White House.</u> Parsippany, NJ: Dillon Press, 1996.

Harness, Cheryl. <u>Ghosts of the White House</u>. New York: Simon & Schuster Books, 1998.

Harvey, Miles. <u>Presidential Elections</u>. Chicago: Childrens Press, 1995.

Harvey, Miles, <u>Women's Voting Rights</u>. Chicago: Childrens Press, 1996.

Hines, Gary. <u>A Christmas Tree in the White House</u>. New York: Henry Holt & Co., 1998.

Hofmann, Nancy Gendron. <u>How the U.S. Government Works</u>. Emeryville, CA: Ziff-Davis Press, 1995.

"James and Dolley Madison," <u>Cobblestone</u>, March, 1996.

Kane, Joseph Nathan. <u>Facts About The Presidents</u>. New York: The H. W. Wilson Company, 1993.

Leiner, Katherine. <u>First Children, Growing Up in the White House</u>. New York: Tambourine Books, 1996.

<u>Living White House, The</u>. Washington, DC: White House Historical Association with the cooperation of the National Geographic Society, 1996.

Maestro, Betsy and Giulio Maestro. <u>The Voice of the People, American Democracy in Action.</u> New York: Lothrop, Lee & Shepard Books, 1996.

Parker, Nancy Winslow. <u>The President's Cabinet and How It Grew</u>. New York: Harper Collins Publishers, 1991.

Pascoe, Elaine. <u>First Facts About The Presidents</u>. Woodbridge, CT: Blackbirch Press, Inc., 1996.

Phillips, Louis. Ask Me Anything About the Presidents. New York: Avon Books, 1994.

Provensen, Alice. The Buck Stops Here: The Presidents of the United States. New York: HarperCollins Publishers, 1995.

Quiri, Patricia Ryon. The White House. New York: Franklin Watts, 1996.

Reit, Seymour. Growing Up in the White House. New York: Macmillan, 1968.

Rowan, Roy, and Brooke Janis. First Dogs: American Presidents and Their Best Friends. Chapel Hill, NC: Algonquin Books of Chapel Hill, 1997.

Sandler, Martin W. Presidents. New York: HarperCollins Publishers, 1995.

Sherrow, Victoria. The Big Book of U.S. Presidents. Philadelphia: Courage Books, 1994.

Sorensen, Lynda. Presidents Day. Vero Beach, FL: The Rourke Press, Inc., 1994.

Sorensen, Lynda. The White House. Vero Beach, FL: The Rourke Press, Inc., 1994.

Spies, Karen. Our Presidency. Brookfield, CT: The Millbrook Press, 1994.

Stein, R. Conrad. The Story of the Powers of the President. Chicago: Childrens Press, 1985.

Suid, Murray and Marilynn G. Barr. How to Be President of the U.S.A. Palo Alto, CA: Monday Morning Books, 1992.

Steins, Richard. Our Elections. Brookfield, CT: The Millbrook Press, 1994.

Seuling, Barbara. The Last Cow on the White House Lawn and Other Little Known Facts about the Presidency. New York: Doubleday, 1978.

Sullivan, George. Mr. President: A Book of U.S. Presidents. Revised edition. New York: Scholastic, 1992.

Sullivan, George. How The White House Really Works. New York: Lodestar Books, E. P. Dutton, 1989.

Waters, Kate. The Story of the White House. New York: Scholastic, 1991.

Weber, Michael. The Complete History of Our Presidents. 13 volumes. Vero Beach, FL: Rourke Corp., 1997.

Weizmann, Daniel and Jack Keely. Take a Stand! Los Angeles: Price Stern Sloan, 1996.

The White House: An Historic Guide. Washington, D.C.: The White House Historical Association, 1994.

Learning about Congress and the Legislative Process with *House Mouse, Senate Mouse*

Story Synopsis

House Mouse, Senate Mouse is about an imaginary society of mice in the United States with a government that operates like our own. Just as we elect members of the House of Representatives and the Senate, the mice elect a Congress as well. This imaginary mouse House and Senate works in a miniature mouse Capitol building, on Capitol Hill in Washington, D.C.

The story begins in a second grade mouse classroom in "Moussouri." The teacher, Miss Tuftmouse, gives her students an assignment. The children must write a letter to Congress about an important issue. The children's letter asks Congress to pass a new law – a law to establish a National Cheese for the mouse nation. Miss Tuftmouse mails the letter to the Capitol, where the "Postmouster" delivers it to Longworth McMouse, the "Squeaker of the House," the leader of the House mice. Longworth shares the letter with his counterpart in the Senate, Russell Mouse Bennett, the "Mouse-jority Leader." They discuss the idea and agree it is a good one. They send it on its way through the legislative process.

The process begins at the Library of Congress, where researchers work on the language and content of the bill. From there, the proposal goes to a committee, where it is debated, discussed and approved. It is sent to the floor of each chamber, the Senate and the House, for consideration. But as in real-life politics, the proposed legislation is caught up in controversy – mice citizens and lawmakers cannot agree on which cheese should be designated the National Cheese.

To save the bill, the Squeaker and the Mouse-jority leader convene a meeting of the brightest minds in the mouse Congress. One of them, Senator Thurmouse, evokes the image of the mouse Founding Fathers, who relied on compromise to create the mouse nation. Thurmouse proposes a compromise on the National Cheese bill – he suggests that while every mouse likes different cheeses, the National Cheese should be <u>American</u> cheese because, despite their differences, they are all <u>Americans</u>. The compromise is accepted and passed by the full House and Senate. The bill goes to the mouse President, who signs it the next day. Back in Moussouri, Miss Tuftmouse and her class watch the signing ceremony on television and are pleased with their role in creating a new law.

The last two pages of the book are historical notes for parents and teachers. They include a brief overview of the construction and architecture of the Capitol and of how a bill becomes a law.

Before Reading
Teachers should tell students that they will be reading about a mouse Congress. Be sure to explain that this body is <u>imaginary</u>, that it exists only in our minds. But explain that by reading about the mouse Congress, the National Cheese bill and Miss Tuftmouse's class, students will learn about the legislative process that works in the real Congress in Washington, D.C.

Also inform students that some of the titles in the book are puns of titles of real people in Congress. The puns are intended to make the story more entertaining:

"Squeaker of the House" = Speaker of the House
"Mouse-jority Leader" = Majority Leader
"Postmouster"= Postmaster

Teachers can also prepare for the story by asking students what they already know about Congress and the legislative process: What does the Congress do? Who is elected to Congress? What is a law? With whom does Congress work to create laws?

Teachers can also discuss the author and illustrator, Peter and Cheryl Barnes, their books and backgrounds. Teachers can point out that the Barneses live outside of Washington, D.C., have met many members of Congress and have been to the Capitol many times. In fact, Peter was a television news reporter who covered Congress as part of his job.

Teachers should also be sure to tell students to study the detailed illustrations in the story, which accurately depict the architecture and furnishings of the Capitol, and should alert students to listen for the rhyme and rhythm of the text.

During Reading
It is important that *House Mouse, Senate Mouse* be read aloud to the students so that they can listen to the rhyme and rhythm of the words as well as attend to the story line.

Re-reading

Reread the book to the entire class or small groups OR use multiple copies of the book and have students work in small groups so that each student can have a copy of the book. For older readers, partner reading may be appropriate.

A second read-aloud session is suggested with a specific focus for the listeners, either for the entire class or for cooperative learning groups. Possible focus directions are:

    What are the two major bodies that make up Congress?

    What is the major responsibility of Congress?

    Who are the leaders of Congress?

    What is a compromise?

    How are laws created?

    What are some of the important rooms in the Capitol?

After Reading

Help students brainstorm a list of what they have learned about Congress, the Capitol and the legislative process. These facts may be recorded by students on the "Facts" sheet (see Appendix 3). Work with students to create an outline of the facts, grouping ideas that belong together. Give each group of facts a heading and put them in logical order to create an outline. Possible headings include steps in making a law, how to compromise, etc. Other headings will be initiated by students' ideas.

After students have created their outlines, help students summarize the information. Facts can be presented in organized presentations that include the most important points learned. Presentations can be a group project or individual effort, oral or written, and prepared in a variety of ways. The final product may include reports, charts or graphs, dramatization, audio/visual format, etc.

Activities

These suggested activities can be done by students individually, in cooperative groups and/or by the whole class. Select the activities most appropriate for your grade level and students. All appendices may be reproduced on paper, transparency or any other classroom medium.

1. Character Study

    ★ Write a character sketch using adjectives to describe the character.

    ★ Use a "Descriptive Organizer" for one of the characters being studied (see Appendix 4).

    ★ List a main character and supporting characters.

    ★ Use a "Character Study Organizer" to list character traits and important events related to the Squeaker and Mouse-jority Leader (see Appendix 5).

    ★ Compare and contrast the Squeaker and Mouse-jority Leader, using the "Compare/Contrast Organizer" (see Appendix 6).

2. *Charts and Diagrams*

★ Make a chart or diagram of "How a Bill Becomes a Law" or use a "Sequential Organizer" to show the steps (see Appendix 16).

★ Complete a "Story Map" for the book (choose Appendix 7 or 8).

★ Retell the story using the "Sequential Organizer," "Step by Step" or "Sequence Chain" to list main or important events (see Appendices 16, 17 & 18).

★ Complete the *House Mouse, Senate Mouse* crossword puzzle (see Appendix 21).

3. *Poetry and writing*

★ Write a rhyming poem about mice or a poem with a mouse character.

★ Write an Acrostic poem, using words like "Mice," "Congress," "House," etc. (see Appendix 9).

★ Write a Diamante (Diamond) poem, a Cinquain or a free form poem, using words generated from the book (see Appendices 10 & 11 for samples).

★ Make a list of words describing the Congress. Use these words to write a patriotic poem.

★ Create some new "plays on words" like the ones found in the book, such as "Squeaker of the House," which is a play of words of "Speaker of the House." Create plays on words using other animals, such as dogs or cats.

4. *Drawing*

★ Draw a mouse character (see Appendices 12, 13, & 14).

★ Make a mouse bookmark (see Appendix 15 for pattern).

★ Draw a cartoon, using mice characters. Older students can learn about political cartoons and create their own. Younger students will enjoy creating a cartoon for the comics section of the newspaper.

5. *Discourse*

★ Come up with an idea for a bill in Congress. Research it in your school library. Write the "legislative language" in one paragraph. Create a committee to examine the proposal. Select a committee chairman to manage a debate about it. Give each student on the committee a limited amount of time (controlled by the chairman and a timekeeper) for making statements and asking questions about the proposal. Select students to be "witnesses" who research the proposal and discuss it before the committee and answer questions. Allow the committee members to vote on the proposal.

★ Hold a mock debate in the House or Senate. Select a Speaker of the House or a President of the Senate to oversee the debate. Students on each side select a leader to lead debate on each side. Give arguments for and against the bill. Vote after debate. Students can use the "Pro/Con Organizer" to formulate arguments (see Appendix 19).

★ Work out a compromise on a proposed bill. Discuss the concept of compromise. Vote on the compromise and send it to the President for signature. Select a student to act as President and hold a "signing ceremony" for the bill.

Note: Teachers may want to create a one- or two-week module out of this role playing exercise. Give students a day or two to come up with their idea for a bill and research it. Give them a day or two to hold committee hearings, to hold "floor debate" the next day, etc.

6. News
★ Write a news story about a real or imagined bill passed by Congress and signed into law by the President.

★ Prepare a news bulletin or brief related to the bill for a television news broadcast.

★ Prepare a list of questions for an interview with the Senator or House member who sponsored the bill.

★ Hold a mock press conference, with some students playing members of Congress and others playing reporters.

★ Prepare a list of questions for an interview with Peter and Cheryl Barnes about *House Mouse, Senate Mouse.*

7. Correspondence
★ Write a letter to your local newspaper about an issue or a law.

★ Write a letter to the Speaker of the House or the Senate Majority Leader about an important issue or an idea for a new law at the address below.

★ Write your member of the House of Representatives or your Senator about an issue or an idea for a new law.

To a Senator:
The Honorable (full name)
United States Senate
Washington, D.C. 20510

To a Representative:
The Honorable (full name)
United States House of Representatives
Washington, D.C. 20515

The phone number of the Capitol switchboard is (202) 224-3121

8. Research Topics

★ Research the responsibilities of Congress as described in the Constitution (Article I).

★ Research the history of the U. S. Capitol.

★ Research the history of one of the major rooms in the Capitol. Compare the drawing of that room in the book to an actual photograph of the room. How is it the same as the drawing? How is it different from the drawing?

★ Research the different types of leaders in Congress: The Speaker of the House, the President of the Senate, the majority and minority leaders in each chamber.

★ Research your current member of the House of Representatives or your current Senator. Have students brainstorm a list of sources and important facts that they want to include before they begin their research.

★ Research a famous member of Congress from the past:

Rep. Joe Cannon (noted Speaker)

Sen. Hattie Caraway (first elected female Senator)

Rep. Henry Clay (noted Speaker)

Sen. Everett Dirkson (noted Senator)

Sen. Rebecca Felton (first appointed female Senator)

Rep. Joseph Marion Hernandez (first Hispanic-American member of the House)

Sen. Octaviano A. Larrazolo (first Hispanic-American Senator)

Rep. Nicholas Longworth (noted Speaker)

Rep. Joseph H. Rainey (first African-American member of the House)

Rep. Jeannette Rankin (first female House member)

Rep. Sam Rayburn (noted Speaker)

Sen. Hiram R. Revels (first African-American Senator)

Note: Biographical information on these members can be found through the House and Senate websites, listed below.

9. Contact your Senator or your member of the House to gain first hand knowledge of his/her job responsibilities. (Search the House and Senate websites listed below for names.)

10. Arrange a field trip to the U. S. Capitol.

11. As an individual exercise, each student can prepare an oral or written presentation on what he or she would do if he or she were a member of Congress. The report should include a proposal for a new law that the student would sponsor as a member.

12. As an individual exercise, students may respond to the book using the "Pro/Con Organizer" to list reasons why they like or dislike the book (see Appendix 19).

13. Research Washington, D.C., the nation's capital. In every nation, the capital is a special place. It is usually full of unique and historic buildings, representing the best architecture of a nation. Identify the special buildings in Washington. Compare Washington to your town or city, or to your county seat or state capital. Use photographs from newspapers, magazines or books. What are the special buildings in your town, city, county seat or state capital?

Note to teachers: You may consider organizing a field trip to the important buildings in your locality, or to your county seat or state capital to supplement this research. You may also want to compare only one Washington structure with the corresponding structure in your community, such as the White House with City Hall, the Supreme Court with the county courthouse, etc.

For all research projects, encourage students to use a variety of sources, including books, magazines, newspapers, special reference materials, historical records, personal tours/interviews, brochures, the Internet, CD-ROMs, E-mail contacts, etc.

Websites

www.4government.com
An all-purpose website for the different branches of government. It includes links to most major websites for the three main branches, as well as additional links to major government departments and agencies (under "Executive Branch"), to state and local government sites, and to sites for major historical documents, including the Constitution and the Bill of Rights. It also offers links to international governing institutions, such as the United Nations.

www.senate.gov
The home page of the Senate. It includes information on all Senators, links to their websites, a daily schedule of legislative events, an explanation of how the Senate works, a history of the body and a review of major Senate artworks.

www.house.gov
The home page of the House. It includes information on all Representatives, links to their websites, search functions by name and state, an explanation of the legislative process and legislative schedules.

www.aoc.gov
The home page of the Architect of the Capitol. It includes a history of the construction of the Capitol, details on architectural features and historic spaces, and the art of the building.

www.uschs.org

The home page of the United States Capitol Historical Society. It includes an interactive tour of the Capitol, historic 19th century photos (stereographs) of the building and a "feature of the month."

www.clerkweb.house.gov

The website of the Office of the Clerk of the House of Representatives. Lots of information on the history of the House and its work, biographies of past and present members, congressional documents, and a tour of the chamber.

www.congress.org

A non-profit website for learning about and interacting with Congress. It includes a congressional directory, methods for contacting members of Congress, an easy e-mail service to reach members, bill status reports and a "member of the day" feature.

www.dcpages.com

A for-profit website guide to Washington, D.C., loaded with information about our nation's capital, including tourist information and a search engine for D.C. attractions and events.

www.congresslink.org

An educational website about Congress developed for teachers and for classroom applications by the non-profit Dirkson Congressional Center in Perkin, Il. It includes special exercises and research activities, mainly for secondary and high school students. But it includes glossaries and other features that may be helpful in elementary classrooms.

www.nara.gov

The website of the National Archives (formally known as the National Archives and Record Administration). It offers access to many federal documents, but the main attraction for kids is the Online Exhibition Hall, which includes the Constitution, the Bill of Rights and the Declaration of Independence. There is also a Digital Classroom.

Check for Understanding

By the end of studying *House Mouse, Senate Mouse*, students should have a basic understanding of the following:

★ What a "law" is.
★ The major responsibility of Congress, which is to create laws.
★ How the House and Senate work together.
★ The meaning of the term "compromise" and its importance in making laws in a diverse nation.
★ Some of the important rooms in the Capitol and how they are used.

Glossary

Bill – a proposed law.

Capital – the city in a state or nation that is the center of government; in the U.S., Washington, D.C.

Capitol – the building where a legislature meets; in the U.S., the meeting place of Congress.

Committee – a group of selected lawmakers assembled to review and consider proposed legislation.

Compromise – a settlement of a dispute in which opposing groups or parties remove their differences by concessions and achieve mutual satisfaction.

Congress – the legislative branch of the federal government, consisting of the House of Representatives and the Senate.

Constitution – the plan of government adopted by Founding Fathers that establishes the basic law and structure of the U.S. government.

Congress – the legislative branch of government, consisting of the House of Representatives and the Senate.

Congressperson – a member of the House of Representatives.

Floor – the area in each chamber of Congress where members sit to consider legislation, hear speeches and conduct other official business.

House of Representatives – the larger, "lower" house of Congress, with 435 members elected every two years.

Law – a rule of conduct or behavior formally recognized by a society and enforced by legal authorities.

Majority Leader – in the Senate, the head of the party in power and the principal administrator of Senate business; in the House, the second highest ranking leader of the party in power, behind the Speaker.

Republic – a government in which the ultimate power rests in the hands of citizens, who are entitled to vote and elect representatives responsible to them and governing according to law.

Rotunda – the large round, domed, ornately decorated room in the center of the Capitol.

Senate – the smaller, "upper" body of Congress, with 100 members elected every six years.

Senator – a member of the Senate.

Speaker of the House – the leader of the party in power in the House and the principal administrator of House business.

Bibliography/Resources, Related Reading

"A Historical Look at Washington, D.C." Cobblestone, January, 1996.

Greene, Carol. Congress. Chicago: Childrens Press, 1985.

Hilton, Suzanne. A Capital Capital City, 1790-1814. New York: Atheneum, Macmillan Publishing Company, 1992.

Maestro, Betsy and Giulio Maestro. The Voice of the People, American Democracy in Action. New York: Lothrop, Lee & Shepard Books, 1996.

Russell, Elizabeth. Our Nation's Capital. New York: Scholastic Professional Books, 1996.

Santella, Andrew. The Capitol. Chicago: Childrens Press, 1995.

Stein, R. Conrad. The Powers of Congress. Chicago: Childrens Press, 1995.

Steins, Richard. Our National Capital. Brookfield, CT: The Millbrook Press, 1994.

We, the People, The Story of the United States Capitol, Its Past and Its Promise. Washington, DC: The United States Capitol Historical Society, 1963.

Weber, Michael. Our Congress. Brookfield, CT: The Millbrook Press, 1994.

Weizmann, Daniel and Jack Keely. Take a Stand! Los Angeles: Price Stern Sloan, 1996.

Learning about the Supreme Court and the Judicial Process With *Marshall, the Courthouse Mouse*

Story Synopsis

Marshall, *the Courthouse Mouse* is about an imaginary society of mice in the United States with a government that operates like our own. Just as we have a Supreme Court, the mice have a Supreme Court. This imaginary mouse Court works in a miniature Supreme Court in Washington, D.C.

The story begins with the opening of the term of the mouse Supreme Court. The reader meets the nine members of the Court, led by Chief Justice Marshall J. Mouse. The story explains that the Supreme Court is just one of many types of courts found throughout the country. Each court has a judge in charge; many courts also operate with lawyers and juries.

The judicial system exists to ensure that the nation's laws are obeyed. There are many types of laws children may be familiar with, such as wearing a seat belt in a car and wearing a bicycle helmet while riding a bike. But there is one group of laws that rise above all others – those laid down in the Constitution and the Bill of Rights. It is the Supreme Court's responsibility to enforce and protect these special laws, which declare the most basic rights in a society, such as the right to free speech and the right to vote.

The story then explains that some laws are sometimes unclear or even unconstitutional! The mice know this well, for their Congress passed a law that requires mice to eat the same cheese on a given day – this law said for example, that all mice had to eat cheddar cheese on Sunday. Some mice favored this law, but other mice thought it wrong. The opponents felt they should be able to eat any cheese they want on any day they choose. How is this disagreement settled? By the mouse Supreme Court, because the issue is big and important and concerns a question of Constitutional rights.

The case goes to the Court through the petition process. Then there are oral arguments by lawyers before the justices. As they proceed, the justices rely on their clerks, or researchers, for help. Clerks do much of their research on a case in the beautiful Court library. As they do their work, the justices meet in private to talk about cases.

In the cheese case, Chief Justice Marshall convinces his fellow justices that the cheese law is unconstitutional and must be struck down because it denies mice a fundamental liberty to pick any cheese they want to eat. The other justices agree. They write their decision in a formal opinion, which is released (handed down) from the bench and announced to the public. That night, at tables across the land, mouse families enjoy the cheese of their choice for dinner.

The last two pages of the book feature historical notes for parents and teachers. They give students a brief overview of the architecture and construction of the Court; of the two real-life Marshalls who inspired the title of the book, John and Thurgood, and of how the Court hears a case.

Before Reading
Teachers should tell students that they will be reading about a mouse Supreme Court. Be sure to explain that this court is <u>imaginary,</u> that it exists only in our minds. But explain that by reading about the mouse Court, students will learn about the judicial process that works in the real Supreme Court in Washington, D.C.

Teachers can also prepare for the story by asking students what they already know about the Supreme Court and the judicial process: What does the Court do? Who is appointed to the Court? What is a law?

Teachers can also discuss the author and illustrator, Peter and Cheryl Barnes, their books and backgrounds. Teachers can point out that the Barneses live outside of Washington, D.C., have met members of the Court and have been to the Court many times. In fact, Peter was a television news reporter who covered the Supreme Court as part of his job.

Teachers should also be sure to tell students to study the detailed illustrations in the story, which accurately depict the architecture and furnishings of the Court building in Washington, and should alert students to listen for the rhyme and rhythm of the text.

During Reading
It is important that *Marshall, the Courthouse Mouse* be read aloud to the students so that they can listen to the rhyme and rhythm of the words as well as attend to the story line.

Re-reading
Reread the book to the entire class or small groups OR use multiple copies of the book and have students work in small groups so that each student can have a copy of the book. For older readers, partner reading may be appropriate.

A second read-aloud session is suggested with a specific <u>focus</u> for the listeners, either for the entire class or for cooperative learning groups. Possible <u>focus</u> directions are:

    Who sits on the Supreme Court?

    What is the major responsibility of the Court?

    What is a law?

    How does the Court hear a case?

    What are some of the important rooms in the Court building?

After Reading

Help students brainstorm a list of what they have learned about the Court, its building and the judicial process. These facts may be recorded by students on the "Facts" sheet (see Appendix 3). Work with students to create an outline of the facts, grouping ideas that belong together. Give each group of facts a heading and put them in logical order to create an outline. Possible headings include steps in reviewing a case, what a law is, etc. Other headings will be initiated by students' ideas.

After students have created their outlines, help students summarize the information. Facts can be presented in organized presentations that include the most important points learned. Presentations can be a group project, or individual effort, oral or written, and prepared in a variety of ways. The final product may include reports, charts or graphs, dramatization, audio/visual format, etc.

Activities

These suggested activities can be done by students individually, in cooperative groups and/or by the whole class. Select the activities most appropriate for your grade level and students. All appendices may be reproduced on paper, transparency or any other classroom medium.

1. Character Study

    ★ Write a character sketch using adjectives to describe the character.

    ★ Use a "Descriptive Organizer" for character being studied (see Appendix 4).

    ★ List a main character and supporting characters.

    ★ Use a "Character Study Organizer" to list character traits and important events related to Marshall (see Appendix 5).

    ★ Compare and contrast Marshall with a different character from another book, using a "Compare/Contrast Organizer" (see Appendix 6).

2. Charts and Diagrams

    ★ Make a chart or diagram of "How the Supreme Court Hears a Case" or use a "Sequential Organizer" to show the steps (see Appendix 16).

    ★ Complete a "Story Map" for the book (choose Appendix 7 or 8).

    ★ Retell the story using the "Sequential Organizer," "Step by Step" or "Sequence Chain" to list main or important events (see Appendices 16, 17 & 18).

    ★ Complete the Supreme Court crossword puzzle (see Appendix 23).

    ★ Name the current Supreme Court Justices (see Appendix 25).

3. Poetry

★ Write a rhyming poem about mice or a poem with a mouse character.

★ Write an Acrostic poem, using words like "Mice," "Court," "Law," etc. (see Appendix 9).

★ Write a Diamante (Diamond) poem, a Cinquain or a free form poem, using words generated from the book (see Appendices 10 & 11).

★ Make a list of words describing the Supreme Court. Use these words to write a patriotic poem.

4. Drawing

★ Draw a mouse character (see Appendices 12, 13 & 14).

★ Make a mouse bookmark (see Appendix 15).

★ Draw a cartoon, using mice characters. Older students can learn about political cartoons and create their own. Younger students will enjoy creating a cartoon for the comics section of the newspaper.

5, Discourse

★ Make up a case that the court could review and that elementary students would relate to (for example, a law that forbids anyone to have dessert after dinner or to serve hamburgers in restaurants, etc.). Describe the disagreement.

★ Create a mock Supreme Court to hear the dispute. Name nine students to sit on the Court, with one as Chief Justice. Name other students as lawyers to argue the case before the "justices." Students can use the "Pro/Con Organizer" to help formulate the key points of arguments (see Appendix 19).

★ Let the justices "retire" to a corner of the room (a make-believe conference room) to argue over the case among themselves and come to a decision.

★ Have the justices write down their decision and the main reasons behind it in a one-paragraph "opinion" and announce it to the classroom.

Note: Teachers may want to create a one-or two-week module out of the role playing exercise suggested above.

6. News

★ Write a news story about a real or imagined decision handed down by the Court.

★ Prepare a news bulletin or brief related to the decision for a television news broadcast.

★ Prepare a list of questions for an interview with the lawyer who argued one side of the case. (Justices do not grant news interviews on cases they decide.)

★ Hold a mock press conference, with some students playing lawyers who argued the case and other students playing reporters.

★ Prepare a list of questions for an interview with Peter and Cheryl Barnes about *Marshall, the Courthouse Mouse.*

7. Correspondence

★ Write a letter to the Chief Justice of the Supreme Court or another justice for information about the Court and his or her job. Send the letter to:

> The Honorable (full name)
> United States Supreme Court
> 1 First Street NE
> Washington, DC 20543

★ Write a letter to your local newspaper about a case the Court is considering or has recently decided.

8. Research Topics

★ Research the responsibilities of the Court as described in the Constitution (Article III).

★ Research the history of the Supreme Court building in Washington, D.C.

★ Research the history of one of the major rooms in the Court building. Compare the drawing of that room in the book to an actual photograph of the room. How is it the same as the drawing? How is it different from the drawing?

★ Research the justices on the Court or a specific current justice.

★ Research a famous member of the Court from the past or present:

> Oliver Wendell Holmes
> John Jay
> John Marshall
> Thurgood Marshall
> Sandra Day O'Connor
> William Howard Taft
> Earl Warren

★ Find a book or article about an historic court decision in the school library, or a recent court decision, and research and analyze it. Two of the most famous court cases students could study are:

> Marbury v. Madison
> Brown v. Board of Education

9. Arrange a field trip to the Supreme Court in Washington, D.C.

10. As an individual exercise, each student can prepare an oral or written presentation on what he or she would do if he or she were a member of Court. The report should include what issues the student would focus on as a justice.

11. As an individual exercise, students may respond to the book using the "Pro/Con Organizer" to list reasons why they like or dislike the book (see Appendix 19).

12. Research Washington, D.C., the nation's capital. In every nation, the capital is a special place. It is usually full of unique and historic buildings, representing the best architecture of a nation. Identify the special buildings in Washington. Compare Washington to your town or city, or to your county seat or state capital. Use photographs from newspapers, magazines or books. What are the special buildings in your town, city, county seat or state capital?

Note to teachers: You may consider organizing a field trip to the important buildings in your locality, or to your county seat or state capital to supplement this research. You may also want to compare only one Washington structure with the corresponding structure in your community, such as the Supreme Court with the county courthouse, etc.

For all research projects, encourage students to use a variety of sources, including books, magazines, newspapers, special reference materials, historical records, personal tours/interviews, brochures, the Internet, CD-ROMs, E-mail contacts, etc.

Websites

www.4government.com
An all-purpose website for the different branches of government. It includes links to most major websites for the three main branches, as well as additional links to state and local government sites, and to sites for major historical documents, including the Constitution and the Bill of rights. It also offers links to international governing institutions, such as the United Nations.

www.law.cornell.edu/supct
The Cornell University law school's official website for the Court. It includes photos of justices, biographies and a database of court decisions.

www.supremecourthistory.org
The website for the Supreme Court Historical Society. It includes a list of significant oral arguments, a digital library of Court-related information, and more.

Check for Understanding
By the end of studying *Marshall, the Courthouse Mouse*, students should have a basic understanding of the following:
   ★ What a "law" is.
   ★ The major responsibility of the Court.
   ★ How the Court hears and decides a case.
   ★ Some of the important rooms in the Court building and how they are used.

Glossary

Bench – the seat where a judge sits in a court; also, another term for a court.

Bill of Rights – the first ten amendments to the Constitution, spelling out our fundamental liberties, including freedom of speech, of the press and of religion.

Case – a lawsuit or legal action in a court.

Chief Justice – the presiding justice on the Supreme Court, responsible for Court administration and court proceedings.

Clerks – At the Supreme Court, lawyers who assist justices in researching cases and writing legal opinions.

Conference – at the Supreme Court, a private meeting of the Justices.

Constitution – the plan of government adopted by the Founding Fathers that establishes the basic law and structure of the U.S. government.

Jury – an impartial group of people selected in a court to investigate a case and render a decision (verdict) about it.

Justice – Any one of the nine members of the Supreme Court.

Law – a rule of conduct or behavior formally recognized by a society and enforced by legal authorities.

Lawyer – a person formally trained and educated in the law who typically advises on legal matters or represents clients in lawsuits.

Opinion – the written explanation of a decision by the Supreme Court.

Oral arguments – presentations made by lawyers to justices in Supreme Court cases.

Petition – a request to the Court to hear a case.

Term – the period of time, usually about nine months, that the Supreme Court is in session and hears cases.

Unconstitutional – in conflict with the Constitution; unlawful.

Bibliography/Resources, Related Reading

Aaseng, Nathan. Great Justices of the Supreme Court. Minneapolis, MN: The Oliver Press, 1992.

Adler, David and Robert Casilla. A Picture Book of Thurgood Marshall. New York: Holiday House, 1997.

Arthur, Joe. Justice for All: The Story of Thurgood Marshall. New York: Yearling Books, 1995.

Bains, Rae. Thurgood Marshall: Fight for Justice. Mahwah, NJ: Troll Associates, 1993.

Baker, Leonard. John Marshall: A Life In Law. New York: MacMillan, 1974.

Cavan, Seamus. Thurgood Marshall and Equal Rights. Brookfield, CT: Millbrook Press, 1993.

Deegan, Paul J. Supreme Court Book. Edina, MN: Abdo & Daughters, 1992.

Dudley, Mark E. Brown V. Board of Education: School Desegregation. Breekenridge, CO:
    Twenty First Century Books, 1995.

Goldish, Meish. Our Supreme Court. Brookfield, CT: Millbrook Press, 1994.

Greene, Carol. Sandra Day O'Connor: The First Woman on the Supreme Court. Chicago:
    Childrens Press, 1982.

Greene, Carol. The Supreme Court. Chicago: Childrens Press, 1985.

Greene, Carol. Thurgood Marshall: First African American Supreme Court Justice. Chicago:
    Childrens Press, 1991.

Kallen, Stuart A. Thurgood Marshall. Edina, MN: Abdo & Daughters, 1993.

Prentzas, G.S. Thurgood Marshall. Broomall, PA: Chelsea House Publishing, 1994.

Quiri, Patricia Ryan. The Supreme Court (A True Book). Chicago: Childrens Press, 1998.

Stein, R. Conrad. Powers of the Supreme Court. Chicago: Childrens Press, 1995.

Addresses of Cabinet Departments and Websites

Department of Agriculture
14th and Independence Avenue SW
Washington, DC 20250
(202) 720-2791
www.usda.gov

Department of Commerce
15th and Constitution Avenue NW
Washington, DC 20230
(202) 482-2000
www.doc.gov

Department of Defense
1000 Defense, The Pentagon
Washington, DC 20301-1000
(703) 545-6700
www.defenselink.mil

Department of Education
600 Independence Avenue SW
Washington, DC 20202
(202) 401-2000
www.ed.gov

Department of Energy
1000 Independence Avenue SW
Washington, DC 20585
(202) 586-5000
www.doe.gov

Department of Health and Human Services
200 Independence Avenue SW
Washington, DC 20201
(202) 619-0257
www.dhhs.gov

Department of Housing and Urban Development
451 7th Street SW
Washington, DC 20410
(202) 401-0388
www.hud.gov

Department of Interior
1849 C Street NW
Washington, DC 20240
(202) 208-3100
www.doi.gov

Department of Justice
950 Pennsylvania Avenue NW
Washington, DC 20530
(202) 514-2000
www.usdoj.gov

Department of Labor
200 Constitution Avenue NW
Washington, DC 20210
(202) 219-6666
www.dol.gov

Appendix 1

Department of State
2201 C Street NW
Washington, DC 20520
(202) 647-4000
www.state.gov

Department of Transportation
400 7th Street SW
Washington, DC 20590
(202) 366-4000
www.dot.gov

Department of the Treasury
1500 Pennsylvania Avenue NW
Washington, DC 20220
(202) 622-2000
www.ustreas.gov

Department of Veterans Affairs
810 Vermont Avenue NW
Washington, DC 20420
(202) 273-5400
www.va.gov

Graphic Organizers are visual aides for students to develop critical thinking. Visual aides help by giving students visual relationships of ideas, creating patterns that can be used again to clarify or summarize other stories, and developing a story format. Included in this guide are organizers that might be helpful for students' activities. Add to this collection of graphic organizers ones you have used or ones your students have created. It may be appropriate to teach students how to decide which organizer is most useful for a particular task or goal. Helping students link the important pieces that make up the whole will help them with critical and creative thinking skills.

Under each box, identify the department of government

Appendix 2

Facts

Book Title

_____

1 _____   6 _____

2 _____   7 _____

3 _____   8 _____

4 _____   9 _____

5 _____   10 _____

Appendix 3

Descriptive Organizer

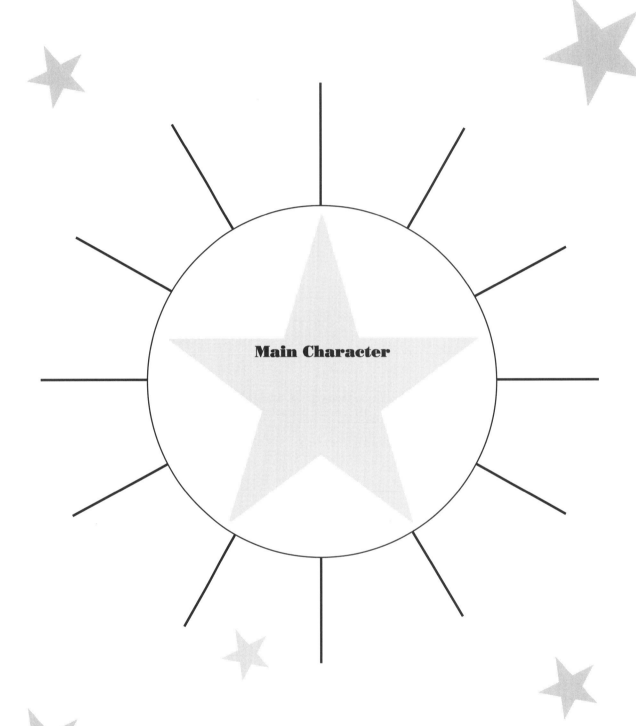

Main Character

Appendix 4

Character Study Organizer

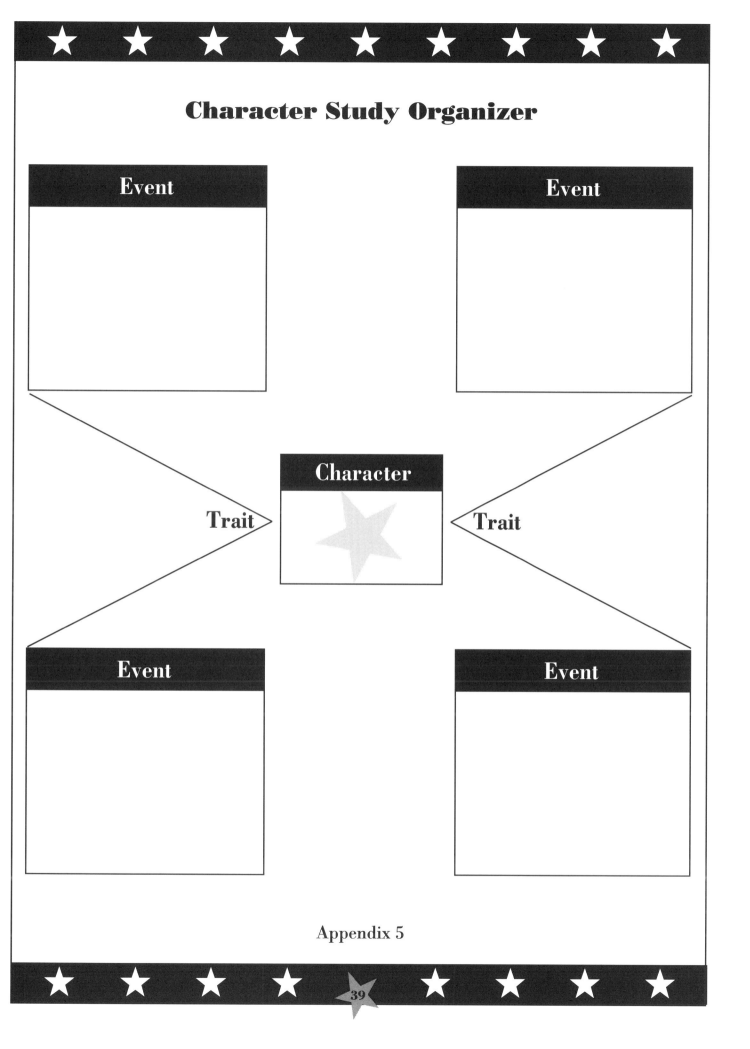

Event

Event

Trait   Character   Trait

Event

Event

Appendix 5

Compare/Contrast Organizer

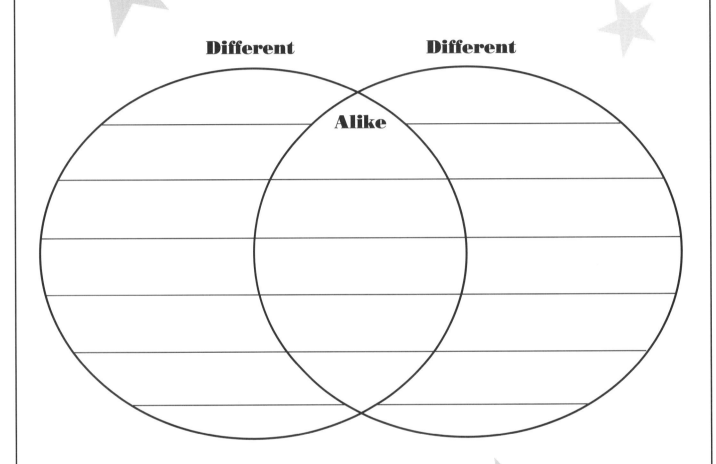

Different   **Different**

Alike

Story Map A

Title: _____

Setting:

Characters: _____ _____

_____ _____

_____ _____

Problem:

Event 1 _____

Event 2 _____

Event 3 _____

Event 4 _____

Event 5 _____

Solution:

Appendix 7

Story Map B

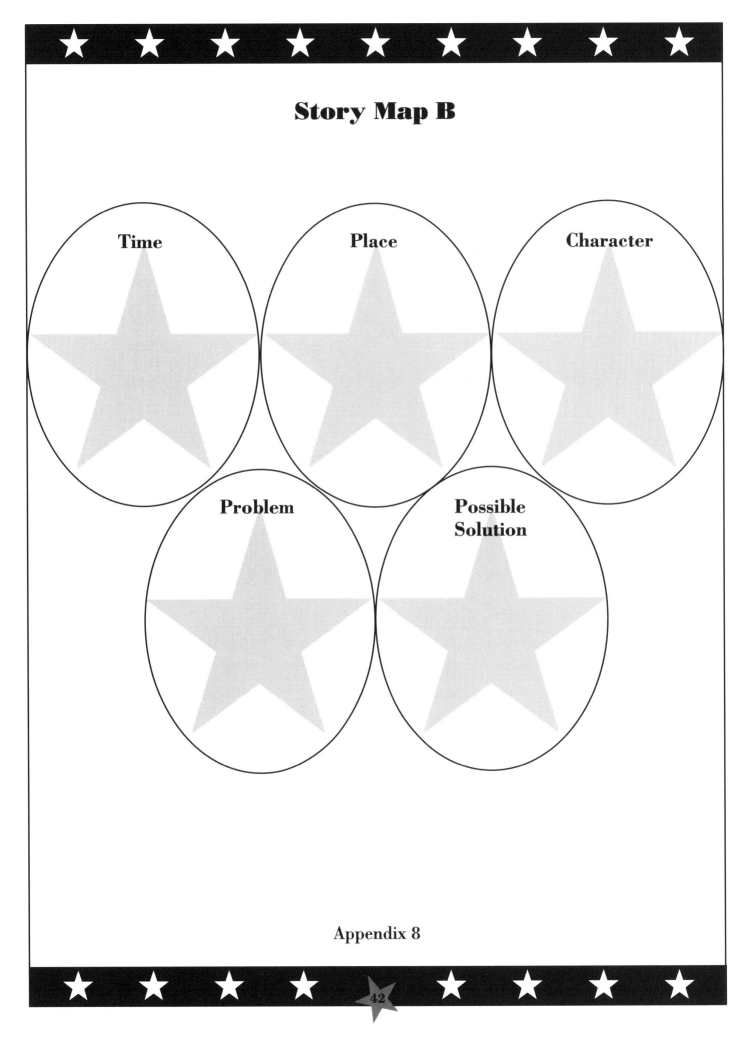

Time

Place

Character

Problem

Possible Solution

Appendix 8

Acrostic Poem

Flying above us

Leading the parade

America

Give a cheer for red, white, and blue

1. Write the letters of a word or name going down instead of across, like FLAG.

2. Begin each line of your poem with the letter already on the line.

3. Describe the word or person in the lines you write.

4. Share your poem with a friend who will proofread for you.

Appendix 9

Diamond Poem

America
young, free
discovering, settling, growing
I love my country
fighting, defending, winning
brave, independent
United States

Read the poem.

Mark off 7 lines on your paper. Draw a diamond around them.

On line 1, write the <u>name</u> of a person, place, or thing – a noun.

On line 2, write 2 words that <u>describe</u> the word on line 1.

On line 3, write 3 <u>action</u> words that tell about the word on line 1.

On line 4, write a 4 word sentence telling how you <u>feel</u> about the word on line 1.

On line 5, write 3 more <u>action</u> words that tell about the word on line 1.

On line 6, write 2 more words that <u>describe</u> the word on line 1.

On line 7, write the first word (noun) again, or write another word that means
   almost the same thing.

Share your poem with a classmate who will help you <u>proofread</u>.

Appendix 10

Word Cinquain Poem

2 words	**The colonies**
4 words	**Fought for their freedom.**
6 words	**Became a nation, strong and brave.**
8 words	**joined in liberty – the United States of America**
2 words	**Our country.**

1. <u>Read</u> the poem.

2. <u>Count</u> the number of words on each line.

3. Mark off <u>5 lines</u> on your paper with the numbers 2,4,6,8,2.
   These numbers tell you how many words to write on each line.

4. Choose a subject for your poem. Start arranging the words of your
   poem to fit the lines.

5. Count the words you have written on each line. Are there 2,4,6,8,2?

6. <u>Recopy</u> your poem neatly.

7. Share your poem with a friend who will help you <u>proofread</u>.

Appendix 11

Woodrow

Appendix 12

Longworth McMouse & Russell Mouse Bennett

Appendix 13

Marshall

Appendix 14

Mouse Bookmark

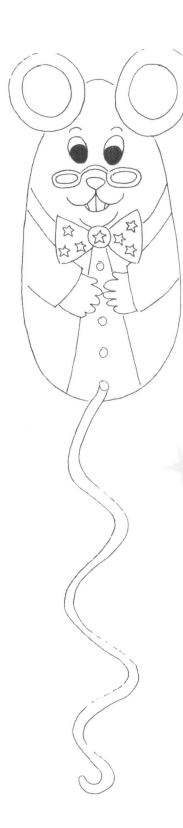

You will need:

★ thin white cardboard

★ pencil

★ scissors

★ permanent black (fine tip) marker

★ colored felt-tip pens

★ grey yarn

★ hole puncher

1. Use pencil to outline Woodrow on thin cardboard. Cut the shape out.

2. Use a permanent black marker to draw in Woodrow image.

3. Use felt tip pens to color in the design.

4. Use hole puncher to attach Woodrow's tail, cut yarn to appropriate length and tie in knot to create tail.

Appendix 15

Sequential Organizer

Appendix 16

Step by Step Sequential Organizer

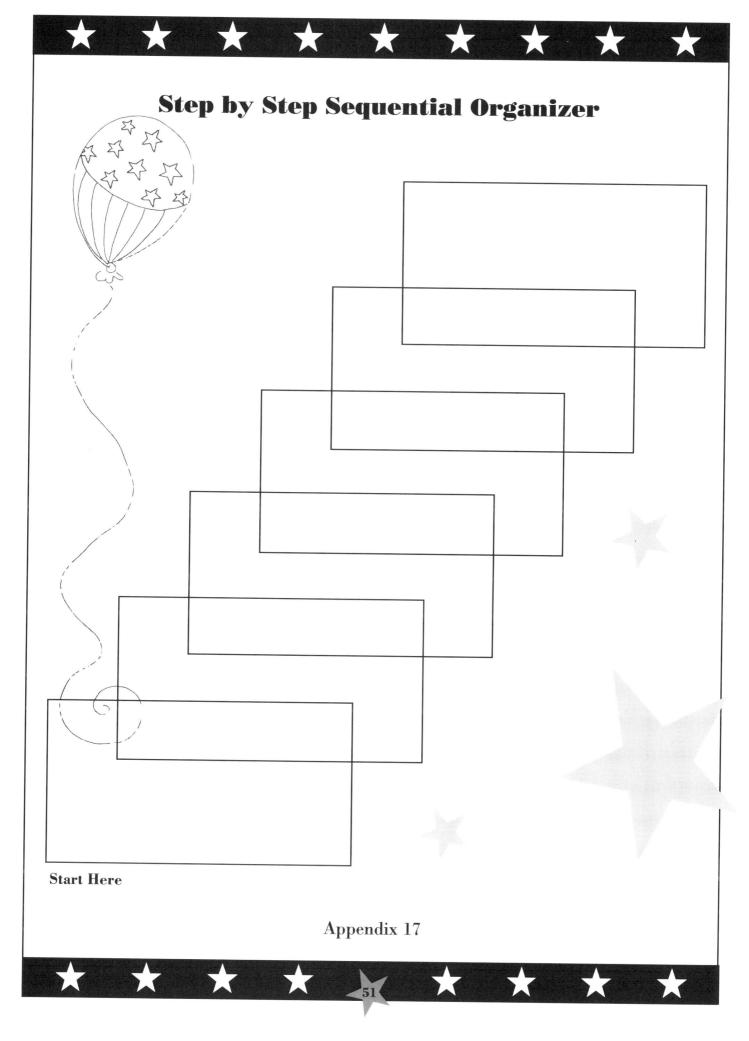

Start Here

Appendix 17

Sequence Chain For

Pro/Con Organizer

1.

2.

3.

4.

5.

1.

2.

3.

4.

5.

Appendix 19

Departments of Government

For each clue, identify the cabinet department that:

ACROSS:

2. Handles the nation's relations with other countries
4. Helps business
6. Helps people get homes
7. Helps make sure people's bodies and minds are healthy
9. Helps workers
10. Is concerned with electricity, oil and other sources of power
11. Is the government's banker and tax collector
13. Helps retired soldiers and sailors and their families (two words)
14. Supervises the nation's parks and a natural places

DOWN:

1. Protects our nation from war or threats by other countries
3. Helps farmers produce our food
5. Helps schools
8. Is concerned with roads, airports and trains
12. Helps defend and protect people from crime and help punish criminals

Answers in Appendix 24

Appendix 20

House Mouse, Senate Mouse

ACROSS:

3. Another word for independence; "let _____ ring"
4. In Washington, D.C., the group of senators and representatives that creates laws
5. A draft of a law presented to Congress for enactment
7. The presiding officer of the House of Representatives
8. The political party that has secured more than half the seats in either the Senate or House
11. A rule that all citizens are to follow
12. A small group of representatives appointed to review a particular issue
13. One of 435 members of Congress who is elected every two years to represent voters in his or her district

Answers in Appendix 24

DOWN:

1. The branch of government that makes laws; this branch is known as the Congress.
2. The _____ of Representatives is the place where many members of Congress meet in the Capitol.
3. The place in each chamber, the Senate and House, where the members speak; opposite of ceiling.
4. The written document stating the fundamental laws of our nation; it was written by our Founding Fathers.
6. Our nation's capital is _____ , D.C.
9. The large, round room that is located in the middle of the Capitol building.
10. A member of Congress who is one of two representatives from each state.
12. The beautiful building that sits on top of a hill in Washington, D.C., where Congress works.

Appendix 21

Woodrow

ACROSS:

2. A President's act of rejecting a proposed law that has been approved by Congress.
4. The last name of George, the first president of the United States.
7. Another term for "armed forces."
8. The President's mansion in Washington, D.C., is called the _____ House.
9. The President oversees the 14 divisions or _____ of government.
12. The _____ room is the largest room in the White House and serves as the main room for concerts, ballets and artistic events.
14. The branch of government that is the presidency.
16. The _____ room is used for formal White House dinners.
17. "Commander in Chief" and "Head of State" are other terms to describe the _____ of the United States.
18. In keeping with tradition, every spring the President and First Lady host the Easter Egg _____ on the South Lawn of the White House.
19. The presidential election is held every _____ years.

DOWN:

1. As Head of State, the President hosts many important functions for _____ leaders from other countries.
2. The abbreviation for "Vice President."
3. As the leader of our military, our President is the "_____ in Chief."
5. All citizens of the United States are _____ citizens.
6. The name of the egg-shaped office of the President located in the west wing of the White House.
10. The department of government that oversees our nations' schools is the Department of _____.
11. The department of government that oversees our money supply and collects taxes is the Department of _____.
13. The wife of the President is also called the _____ Lady.
15. Every four years, citizens vote for a candidate for President in an _____.

Answers in Appendix 24

Appendix 22

Supreme Court

ACROSS:

1. A group of citizens legally chosen to judge a court case.
4. The document stating fundamental laws of our nation; it was written by the Founding Fathers.
7. A formal written request to the Supreme Court to ask it to consider a case.
11. In the judicial system, the person who runs a courtroom in a legal proceeding.
12. A private meeting of the justices for considering and deciding cases.
13. A _____ is the place in a courthouse where legal cases are heard and decided; at the Supreme Court, it is the place the justices meet to hear arguments in cases.
15. A place where books are stored.
16. An assistant to a justice.
19. The last name of two very important past justices of the Supreme Court: first names "John" and "Thurgood."

DOWN:

2. Going against the Constitution.
3. The _____ Justice oversees the work of the Supreme Court.
5. A formal judgment of a case handed down by the Supreme Court.
6. The name for a judge who sits on the Supreme Court
8. The _____ Court is the highest court in the nation
9. Another name for an attorney
10. The third branch of the government, involving courts
14. Another word for independence; "let _____ ring."
17. A rule that all citizens must follow.
18. When lawyers speak about their case at the Supreme Court, they make an _____ argument.

Answers in Appendix 24   **Appendix 23**

Answers for Crossword Puzzles

ANSWERS:
DEPARTMENTS OF GOVERNMENT
ACROSS:
2. State
4. Commerce
6. Housing
7. Health
9. Labor
10. Energy
11. Treasury
13. Veterans Affairs
14. Interior

DOWN:
1. Defense
3. Agriculture
5. Education
8. Transportation
12. Justice

ANSWERS:
HOUSE MOUSE—SENATE MOUSE
ACROSS:
3. freedom
4. Congress
5. bill
7. Speaker
8. majority
11. law
12. committee
13. Representative

DOWN:
1. legislative
2. House
3. floor
4. Constitution
6. Washington
9. rotunda
10. Senator
12. Capitol

ANSWERS:
WOODROW
ACROSS:
2. veto
4. Washington
7. military
8. White
9. departments
12. East
14. Executive
16. State
17. President
18. Roll
19. four

DOWN:
1. foreign
2. VP
3. Commander
5. American
6. Oval
10. Education
11. Treasury
13. First
15. election

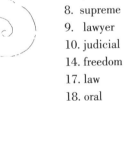

ANSWERS:
SUPREME COURT
ACROSS:
1. jury
4. Constitution
7. petition
11. judge
12. conference
13. courtroom
15. library
16. clerk
19. Marshall

DOWN:
2. unconstitutional
3. chief
5. opinion
6. justice
8. supreme
9. lawyer
10. judicial
14. freedom
17. law
18. oral

Appendix 24

Name the Current Supreme Court Justices

(Teacher supplies answers for current court)

Appendix 25

Structure of the U.S. Government

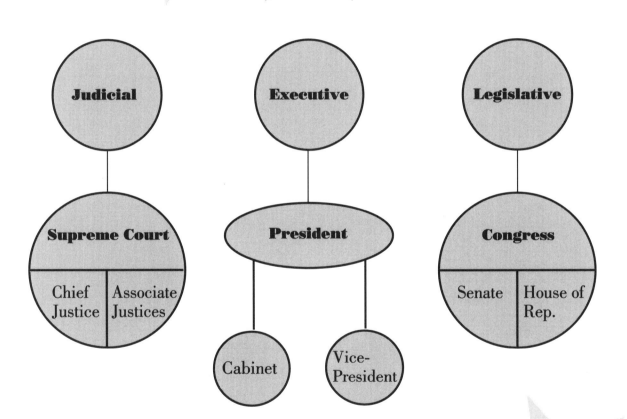

United States
Government

Judicial

Executive

Legislative

Supreme Court

Chief Justice | Associate Justices

President

Cabinet

Vice-President

Congress

Senate | House of Rep.

Appendix 26

NOTES

NOTES

NOTES

NOTES